# Charles Ebling

# From STRENGTH to GRACE to GRATITUDE;

# A Guide for Your Heart Journey

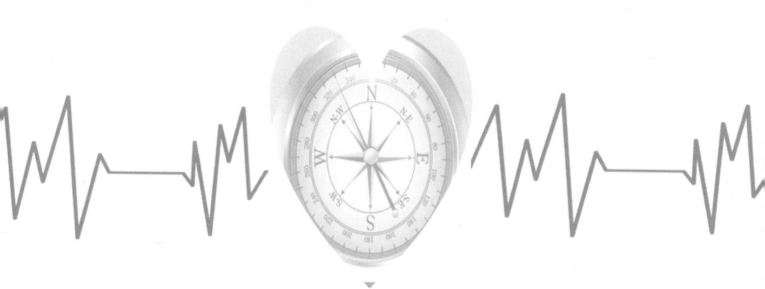

CreateSpace

an Amazon Company

First Edition, June 2018

Book Design by Charles Ebling

Cover Design by Charles Ebling

Library of Congress Cataloging – Publication on file.

Ebling, Charles, birth year 2001
From Strength to Grace to Gratitude; A Guide to your Heart Journey/Charles Ebling 1st ed.
Summary: An Eagle Scout project, this book is about Charles Ebling and his "wishes" for those going through their own heart journey.

ISBN: 978-198-687-9798

1.Ebling, Charles, birth year 2. nonfiction 3. congenital heart defect 4. Boy Scout 5. Newport, Pennsylvania

920 Ebling

This book is dedicated
to all of the heart heroes out there and their families!

and

to my Mom, Carla, my Dad, Ken, and my Sister, Kat;
Because without them I would have never made it this far and
because we all know that a congenital heart defect doesn't just affect the person who has it,
it affects your entire family.

Love you guys!

Well hello there!
My name is Charles.

My family calls me Chaz, and my
friends at school call me Chuck.

I don't really care what you
call me...

as long as you don't call me late for
dinner!

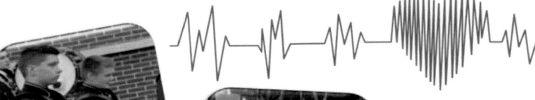

I am currently 17 years old and am a Senior at Newport High School in Newport, Pennsylvania.

Class President, FFA, Student Council, Peer Helpers, Marching Band, where I am the percussion section leader and the lead snare drummer, and our High School musical are just a few activities I participate in at school. I also enjoy spending time with my family, fishing, and anything Star Wars.

I am also active in Boy Scouts – specifically, Newport Troop 222.

There is a lot more, so let's just say that I am an active teenager. But enough about me; this book is for you.

I bet you can't tell from looking at me, but I have a congenital heart defect. I bet you can't tell from looking at you either, am I right?

I was diagnosed with Ebstein's Anomaly when I was 15 months old. I consider myself one of the lucky members of the Zipper Club because I didn't need to have my first open heart surgery until I was 10 years old. Some of us out there had surgeries at just a few days old, maybe even just a few hours old.

Maybe this is your first surgery or maybe it is your 5th surgery; no matter what number this is, I just want you to know that you aren't alone. There are others of us who have been where you are right now.

One of the reasons why I am writing this book is because maybe you are like me and don't want to show anyone your scar, and that is ok. I don't like to show mine much either.

However, when I do, I am proud of it, and I consider it my Badge of Courage.

The other reason I am writing this book is because I want you to know that you are not alone. I know I already said that, but it is really important for you to know.

I want to give you your own Badge of Courage that you can proudly show off. Included with this book is a **key chain/backpack hook** that will be your own personal Badge of Courage that you don't have to be afraid to show off.

As you go through this surgery, each bead on your **key chain/backpack hook** represents a very special wish from me to you:

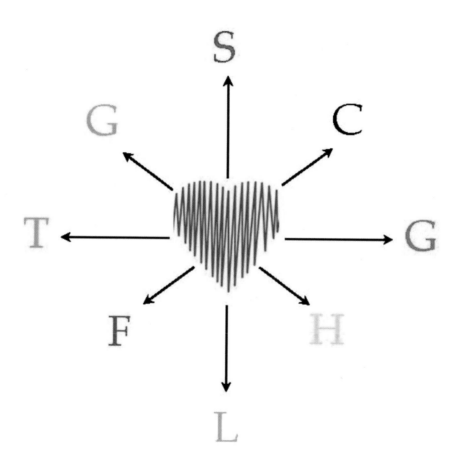

I wish for you STRENGTH.

Not the kind where you can lift a 150lb. barbell, but the kind of strength that you have deep inside you.

It is in you; trust me. I didn't think I had it in me, but when I look back on everything that I have been through; countless tests, two open heart surgeries, two catheterizations, I realize I had to be pretty strong to accomplish all of that.

I wish for you that kind of strength because, in the end, you have a lot more strength than the kid who can bench press 150lbs.

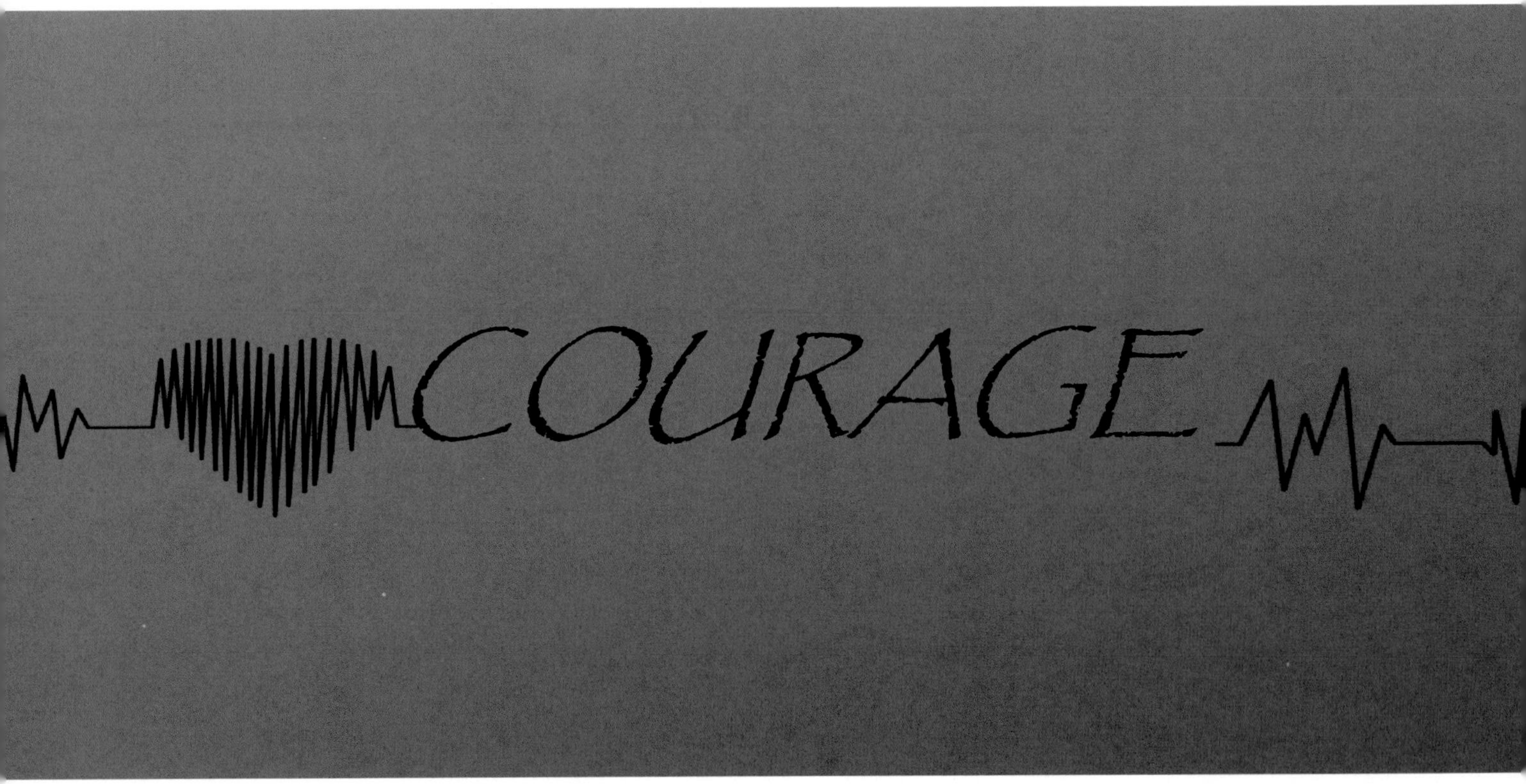
COURAGE

I wish for you **COURAGE**.

Have you ever done something that you were afraid to do, but did it anyway? Maybe it was the first time you rode a bike without training wheels, or the first time you jumped in the deep end of the swimming pool. That is courage!

I can't lie. This is going to be scary. Even if you have been through something like this before, it is always a little scary.

I was 16 when I had my most recent open heart surgery. And I was scared, but in order to feel better, I knew I had to go through with my surgery. My dad told me that it is ok to be scared. Being scared means you are about to do something really, really brave!

The first time I had a Stress Test with the head contraption, I was scared.  It looked scary and it left me no choice  but to breath into that tube.

But, I literally grabbed hold, to the handle, because I didn't want to  be like one of those "American Home Videos" where you go flying off the back, and grabbed my COURAGE as well and took off.

At the end of the stress test I was tired,  but I did it!

Just like me, you can do this.

I don't know if you ever watched the movie _We Bought A Zoo_, but I found this quote that helped me, and I hope it helps you too:

_"All you need is 20 seconds of insane courage and I promise you something great will come of it."_

So when they put on your mask to put you to sleep, take a deep breath, grab onto those 20 seconds of insane courage, and before you know it, you will be waking up, and the scariest part will be over.

I wish for you **GRACE**.

I know, I am a boy, what do I know about Grace? Well, when you are in the hospital and they are poking you, and you are wearing that fashionable gown, you might find that a bit of grace goes a long way.

The last surgery I had, my Mom forgot to pack my underwear. So the first time I could get up and walk around, I had to wear hospital pants that my entire family could have fit into. Baggy, rolled up about 2 feet, my backside still partially hanging out, I was quite the fashion statement.

But you know what? I put my head up and walked down the hallway with grace….and a big smile, because my dad was making jokes about not having underwear on the entire time!

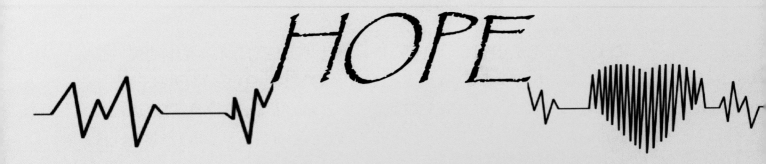

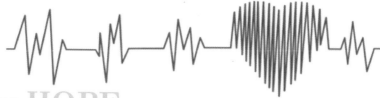

I wish for you HOPE.

I hope that your surgery goes well.

I hope that you have a quick recovery.  I hope that you get to drink some really good slushies while you are in the hospital, they are the best.  The Chef Boyardee Mac and Cheese isn't bad either.  Although my parents might disagree with me.

I have HOPE, and I am passing that HOPE along to you, that researchers will one day allow our doctors to tell us that this is the last surgery we will need because they have come up with a valve, stent or procedure that will last us the rest of our lives!

How awesome would no more surgeries be!

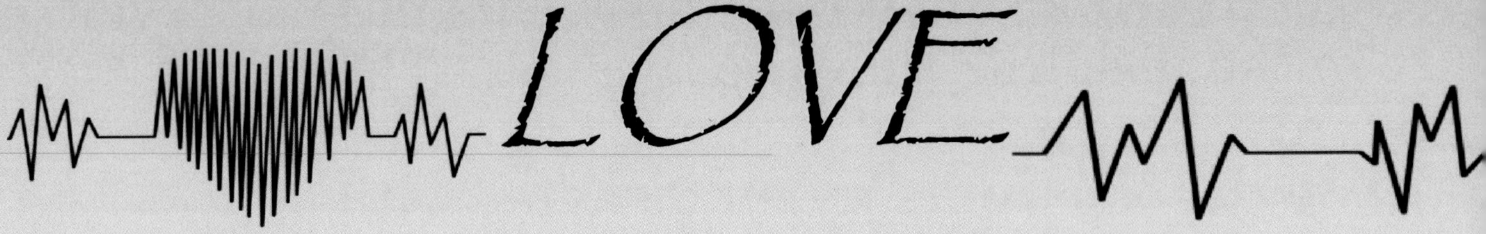
LOVE

I wish for you LOVE.

There are all kinds of love out there. The love you have for your parents. The love you have for your family. The love you have for your friends.

My family likes to have movie nights where we order pizza, wings or both and then watch a movie. One of my favorites is the movie _UP_. My Mom likes it because she says that the first two minutes is the sweetest love story she has ever seen, and no matter how many times she sees it, she still tears up….Moms!

I like <u>Up</u> because of the dog, Dug.  This is what he says the first time he meets Mr. Fredrickson and Russell...

"My name is Dug.  I have just met you, and I love you." ~Dug
Disney/Pixar Movie UP

He reminds me a lot of my dogs, Hunter and Regan.  They love me no matter what.  Basically love is everywhere, and just like Hunter, Regan and Dug, all you have to do is say "yes" when it is given to you.

I know that sometimes talking about love is kind of uncomfortable; who wants a kiss or hug from their sibling or their parents when their friends are around! How un-cool, right?

But I have come to realize that even though I am a big, strong 17 year old, who can act tough most times, having all of that love surrounding me, was one thing that helped me get through all of this, not just the surgery parts, but all of it.

So it is ok to be tough, I know that you are, but don't let that stop you from feeling the love all around you.

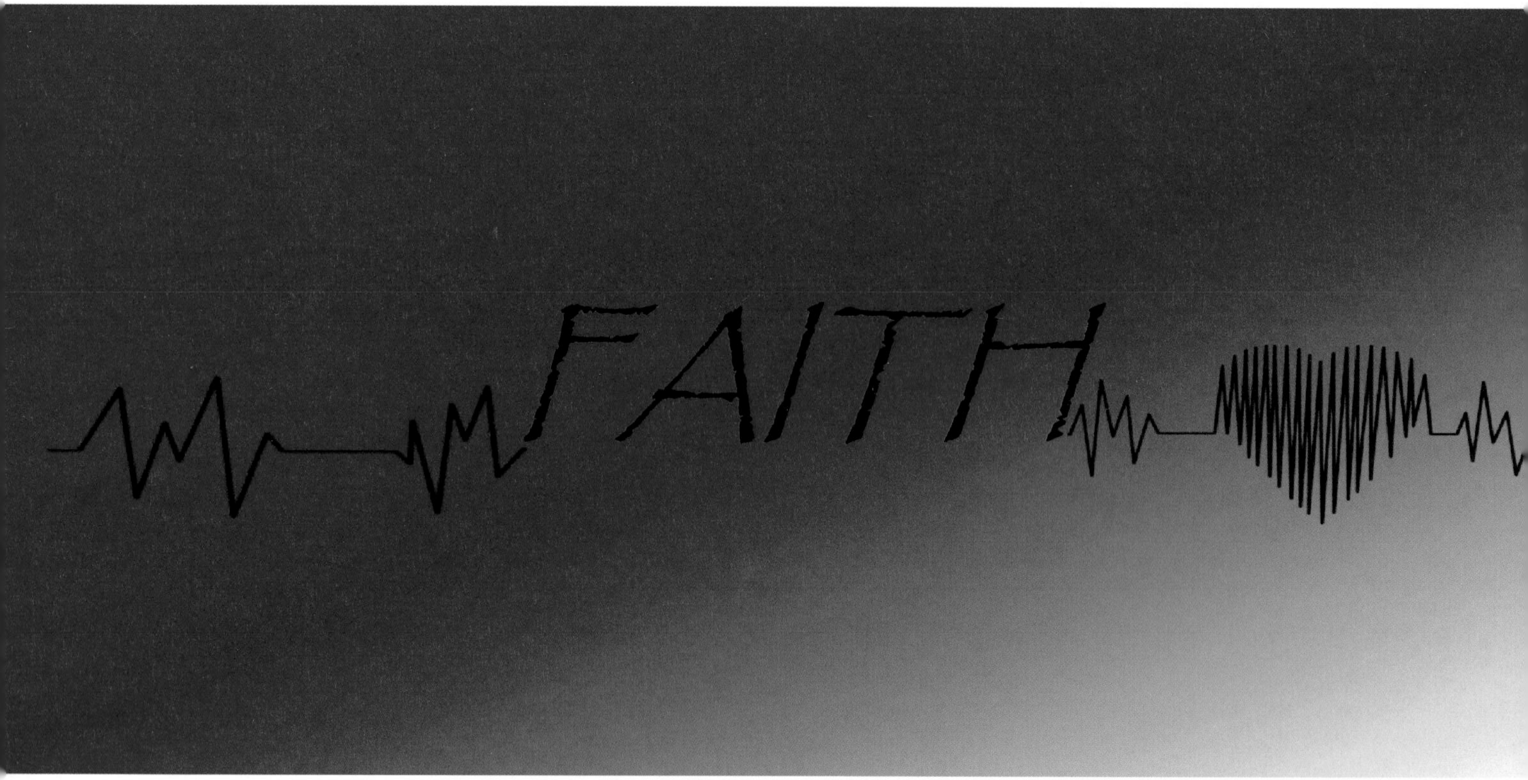
FAITH

I wish for you **FAITH**.

I personally believe in God. I had faith that God was going to see me through my heart journey. Faith is full confidence that you will get through this. No matter if you believe in God, Buddha, Jehovah, Allah, Yahweh, Brahman or a Higher Power or maybe you don't believe at all, that is ok. I still wish for you faith.

Faith is a good thing to have. So whether you have faith in your God, your Higher Power, your parents, your friends, your doctors and nurses, I am glad that I had faith while I was going through my journey. May you have faith during your journey.

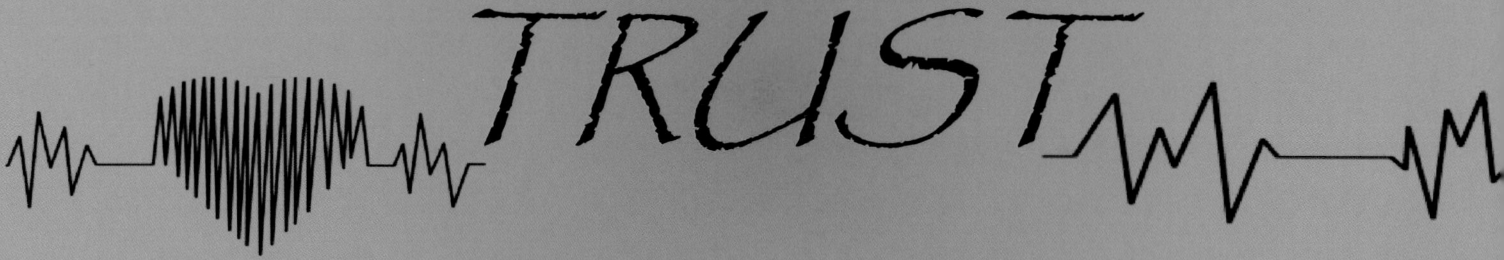
TRUST

I wish for you TRUST.

"All you need is Faith, Trust and a Little Bit of Pixie-Dust" ~Peter Pan

I don't have pixie-dust, but I can wish for you TRUST.

Trust is a hard thing. If only it were as easy as having some pixie-dust!

Your parents, your family, the doctors all want you to feel better. So, like it or not, you have to put your trust in them, and that they will help get you through this journey. They did for me. Trust that they will for you as well.

I wish for you GRATITUDE.

The definition of Gratitude is the quality of being thankful; readiness to show appreciation for and to return kindness.

I know you might be thinking, "with this heart condition what do I have to be thankful for?" Well there is a lot, at least I think so.

We can be thankful for the doctors, nurses, and researchers who continually strive to improve all kinds of medical stuff. It means we get to live a lot longer. If we had been born in a another time, years ago, our lives might have been very different. But thankfully we are here now.

I am thankful for George Lucas, creator of Star Wars. You can ask my family, but I am a little obsessed with anything Star Wars. But it gives me a hobby of collecting Star Wars figures, posters, you name it, I try to collect it. Kind of goofy, I know. It is just one thing that I am thankful for.

Sometimes I know it is hard to find things to be thankful for, especially when you are going through all of this. But all you need to do is look around; there is so much to be thankful for; even the little things count. Sometimes you have to start small before you can see the big stuff.

The second part of the definition is readiness to show appreciation for and to return kindness. So I am going to take this opportunity and thank some very important people who helped me get to where I am today, it is the least I can do. Sorry, this might be a long list. I have had lots of help.

To the doctors, physician assistants and nurses at Hershey Children's Heart Group, especially Dr. Mark Cohen and Marnie O'Donnell, P.A.-C.

Dr. John L. Myers and all of his staff, especially Emily Coulter, P.A.-C. and Kari Paul, P.A.-C.

The awesome nurses at Hershey Medical Center, specifically Nate, Brittany and Katharine. They are some of the best people I have ever had the privilege to meet. They took such wonderful care of me while I was in the hospital. They say that Nurses are just Angels in disguise, and I believe that these three are truly Angels!

Speaking of nurses...thank you to Mrs. Buffington, Mrs. Davis, Mrs. Dessin and especially Mrs. McCollum, the best school nurses a kid could ever ask for! They too are Angels in disguise!

To another group of Angels, the Operating Room Team. A very big thank you to that group of individuals who were in the operating room, doing their thing, so Dr. Myers could do his thing and give me a new heart valve. My family and I have never met them and chances are your family won't meet them either, but they were there and will be there, unseen by us, but without them, our surgeries would not happen. They are unseen heroes and I am so thankful for them.

Mr. Warren Smith, Social Worker, at Hershey Medical Center, for taking such good care of my sister and parents when the surgeon, doctors, and nurses were taking care of me.

The entire Newport School District Family for all of their support and caring over the years. Not only for me, but my mom (who works there, much to my dismay), as well as my sister and my dad. Their support has been unwavering for me and my family.

Mrs. Gleason and Mrs. Schaeffer, two of my most favorite teachers. They were kind enough to give up their time after school to come to my house to help me with my school work when I was out for my surgeries. Because of them, I was able to stay on track, and getting back to school wasn't so difficult.

The school administration and the CAIU and especially Mrs. Lisa Good, our technology administrator, for helping to line up the "robot" for my surgery last year. Being able to see my friends and be in class even when I wasn't in class was so amazing. You have no idea how much that lifted my spirits.

My church family, for all of their prayers and support.

The Newport Marching and Concert Bands, their directors, staff, band boosters, members, and my awesome percussion section. You always made me feel like I belonged, because that is what band is....band is family!

My family; Ma Maw and Granddad; Aunt Lauren and Uncle Andy; Aunt Denise and AJ; Aunt Terri, Uncle Eric, Ericka, and Trey; the Green Families; Uncle Bob and Aunt Joan, Aunt Ada, Aunt Lois and the rest of the Ebling Clan for all your support and prayers.

My other family, those who aren't related by blood, but I consider family and have been there for me every step of the way including Aunt Lois, Uncle Tim, Sarai, Elaine, Jim, Aunt Michelle, Uncle John, Lori, Mr. and Mrs. Shomper, Mr. and Mrs. Bingaman, Mr. and Mrs. Schwaller, Mrs. Mullen and her family, Ms. Sonya, Mr. and Mrs. Mark Miller, Mary Kay Miller, Ms. Carol, Leslie and Aryssa, Mrs. McAlpine, Mrs. Anne Miller, her Daughter and Granddaughter, Kathryn and Audrey and all the countless others I'm sure I am forgetting....I have a very big family!

To my friends, those who have stood by me through thick and thin; Ty, Emily R, Emily D, Jack, Drew, Brianne, Kimmy, Lillie, Allie, Skyelar, Logan, Jamie, Emily B., Sam, Mallory, Chloe, Jozie, Shelby, Dominic, Joel, Xaiver, Noah, Garry, Dalton, Skylar and Ashlyn.

To all the others who I might not have named, but who are just as important: you have come and gone in my life, but you were always there for support.

My Boy Scout Troop, 222 of Newport, the scouts and the leaders...Without your help, my Eagle project would not have become a reality.

Mrs. Wagner, Mrs. Miller, and Mrs. Magee, best English teachers ever, for your help with editing and for all of your caring and support over the years.

My sister Kat. She is a spit fire, and she might be younger than I am, but she has my back.  I am pretty sure she can take on just about anyone who messes with me.

My mom and dad, can't imagine having to go through this without you.  You are my heroes!

Lastly, I am thankful for all of you, my fellow heart heroes.

Because of you, I am not alone in this big world.

From the bottom of my heart, thank you.
I might not know who you are, but when I see your key ring, that will be our little signal that we are heroes in disguise.
Kind of like the Justice League,
only we are the Heart Hero League.

See, you start small and pretty soon you have a big list that fills your heart with GRATITUDE!

Well, that is about it, not really the book I started out to write.  I kind of got stuck half way through, I wanted this to be more than just about my story.

Then one day when I was listening to Tim McGraw's song, "Humble and Kind" it hit me.  The part of the song where he talks about not forgetting to turn back around and make sure you help those coming behind you. That is exactly what I wanted to do.

Just like the song, I felt like I was getting where I was going and wanted to "help the next one in line." I just wasn't sure how to give you something that would be helpful, but I knew it was more than just giving you the details of my story.

So I talked with my Mom, and she told me what I wanted to do sounded a lot like what she does for the prayer shawls she knits for friends and family.

We talked it out some more, and I came up with my list of "wishes" that have gotten me this far in my journey with Ebstein's Anomaly.

I hope you can now carry all of my "wishes" on your heart journey.

Maybe we will meet in the Heart Hero Hall of
Justice one day!

Until then, safe travels on your Heart Journey,
my friend!

*With all the strength, courage, grace,
hope, love, faith, trust
and gratitude.*

*~ Charles*

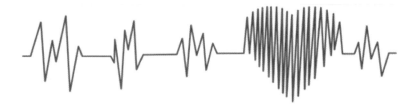

Made in the USA
Middletown, DE
21 March 2022

63000016R00027